Ladybird  Readers

# Dinosaurs

Series Editor: Sorrel Pitts
Text adapted by Sorrel Pitts
Illustrated by Mike Spoor

LADYBIRD BOOKS

UK | USA | Canada | Ireland | Australia
India | New Zealand | South Africa

Ladybird Books is part of the Penguin Random House group of companies
whose addresses can be found at global.penguinrandomhouse.com.
www.penguin.co.uk   www.puffin.co.uk   www.ladybird.com

Penguin
Random House
UK

First published 2016
004

Printed in China

A CIP catalogue record for this book is available from the British Library

ISBN: 978-0-241-25447-9

MIX
Paper from
responsible sources
FSC® C018179

Penguin Random House is committed to a
sustainable future for our business, our readers
and our planet. This book is made from Forest
Stewardship Council® certified paper.

# Dinosaurs

# Contents

Picture words   6

In the past   8

Plants   10

Meat   12

Little dinosaurs   14

Big dinosaurs   16

Strong teeth   18

Big claws   20

Strong dinosaurs   22

Dinosaurs now   24

Activities   26

# Picture words

claws

Triceratops

Tyrannosaurus rex

fight

Diplodocus

Earth

Velociraptor

# In the past

Dinosaurs lived on Earth in the past.

Dinosaurs are not here now.

Dinosaurs lived in the past.

# Plants

## Some dinosaurs ate plants.

Triceratops

plant

Triceratops was a big dinosaur.
It liked eating plants.

11

# Meat

Some dinosaurs liked eating meat. Tyrannosaurus rex was a strong dinosaur. It liked eating meat very much.

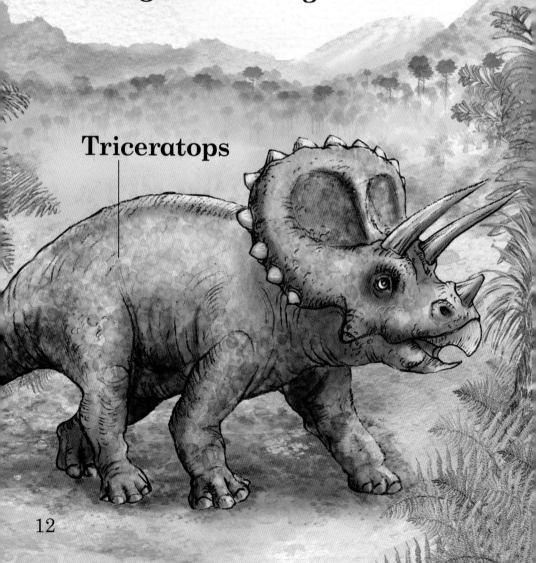

Triceratops

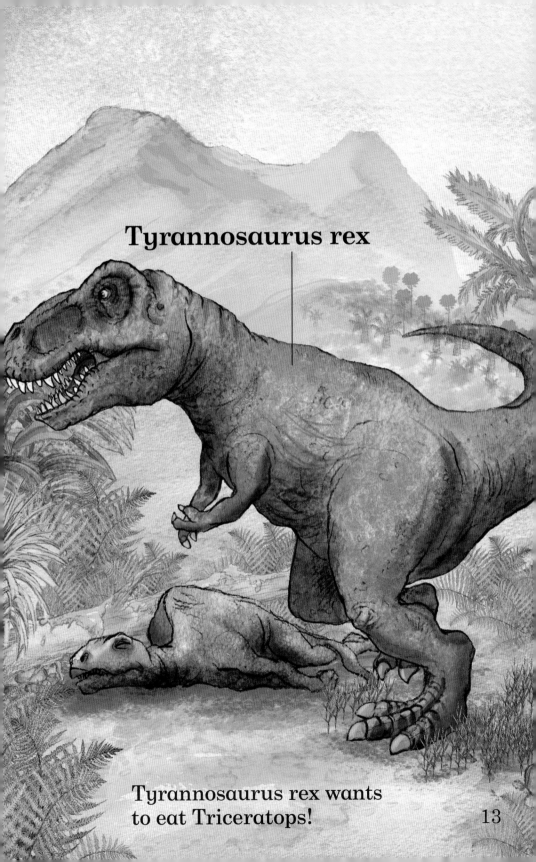

**Tyrannosaurus rex**

Tyrannosaurus rex wants
to eat Triceratops!

# Little dinosaurs

Many dinosaurs were
very small.

Velociraptor

Velociraptor was a small dinosaur.
It liked eating meat, too.

# Big dinosaurs

Some dinosaurs were very big.

Diplodocus was a very, VERY big dinosaur with short legs!

# Diplodocus

Diplodocus liked
eating plants.

## Strong teeth

Some dinosaurs had big, strong teeth in their mouths.

Tyrannosaurus rex had VERY big, strong teeth.

# Tyrannosaurus rex

Tyrannosaurus rex ate meat
with its big, strong teeth.

# Big claws

Some dinosaurs had big claws.

Velociraptor had VERY big, strong claws!

Velociraptor liked fighting
with its strong claws.

claws

# Strong dinosaurs

Some dinosaurs were very strong.

Diplodocus was very big and strong.

Tyrannosaurus rex liked
fighting with its big,
strong teeth.

# Dinosaurs now

Come in here and see many dinosaurs from the past!

You can see lots of dinosaurs in here!

# Activities

The key below describes the skills practiced in each activity.

 Spelling and writing

 Reading

 Speaking

? Critical thinking

 Preparation for the Cambridge Young Learners Exams

**1** **Look and read.**
**Put a** ☑ **or a** ☒ **in the box.**

**1**  This is Diplodocus. ✓

**2**  This is
Tyrannosaurus rex.

**3**  This is Triceratops.

**4**  This is Velociraptor.

**5**  These are claws.

**2** **Look and read. Choose the correct words and write them on the lines.** 📖 ✏️ 🌰

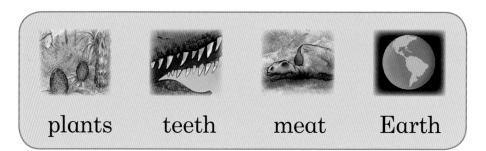

plants    teeth    meat    Earth

1 Dinosaurs lived on  Earth  in the past.

2 Triceratops ate ⸺ .

3 Tyrannosaurus rex ate ⸺ .

4 Tyrannosaurus rex ate with its big, strong ⸺ .

**3** Work with a friend.
Talk about the two pictures.
How are they different? 💬

a

b

**Example:**

In picture a,
Tyrannosaurus rex is
not in front of the trees.

In picture b,
Tyrannosaurus rex
is in front of the trees.

**4** **Write the missing letters.**

Diplodocus

Velociraptor

Triceratops     Tyrannosaurus rex

**1** d i n o s a u r s

**2** D i p l o       c u s

**3** T r i c e r a       s

**4** T y r a n n o       u s  r e x

**5** V e l o c i       t o r

**5** Match the two parts of the sentence. 📖

1 Triceratops

2 Velociraptor

3 Tyrannosaurus rex

4 Diplodocus

**a** had very big, strong teeth.

**b** liked eating plants.

**c** liked eating plants and was a big dinosaur.

**d** was a small dinosaur.

**6** Look at the picture
and read the questions.
Write short answers.

Big dinosaurs

Some dinosaurs were
very big.

Diplodocus was a very,
VERY big dinosaur with
short legs!

Diplodocus

Diplodocus liked
eating plants.

16    17

**1** Did some dinosaurs have big bodies
and little heads?

Yes, they did.

**2** Did some dinosaurs have short legs?

**3** Did Diplodocus eat meat?

# 7 Ask and answer the questions with a friend. 🗨

**a**

**Little dinosaurs**
Many dinosaurs were
very small.

Velociraptor

Velociraptor w
It liked eating

**b**

**Big claws**
Some dinosaurs had big claws.

Velociraptor had VERY big,
strong claws!

Velociraptor liked fighting
with his strong claws.
claws

**1** *Which dinosaur was this?*

*This was Velociraptor.*

**2** What color was it?

**3** Was it a big or a little dinosaur?

**4** What did it use to fight?

**8** **Read the text. Choose the correct words and write them on the lines.** 📖 ✏️ ⬡

| 1 | was | were | are |
|---|-----|------|-----|
| 2 | live | are living | lived |
| 3 | are | were | is |
| 4 | eat | ate | are eating |
| 5 | eat | ate | eating |

Some dinosaurs [1] __were__ big

animals. They [2] _____ on Earth

in the past. Dinosaurs [3] _____

not here now. Some dinosaurs

[4] _____ plants and some

dinosaurs did not. Tyrannosaurus rex

liked [5] _____ meat very much.

**9** **Circle the correct word.**

1 Many dinosaurs were not **big** / **animals**.

2 Velociraptor ate **meat** / **plants**.

3 Diplodocus was a very big dinosaur with **long** / **short** legs.

4 Velociraptor liked fighting with its strong **teeth** / **claws**.

**10** **Work with a friend. Look at the pictures. One picture is different. How is it different?** 🗨

**Example:**

*Picture c is different because it is not in the past.*

**11** **Look at the picture and read the questions. Write complete sentences.**

Meat
Some dinosaurs liked eating meat. Tyrannosaurus rex was a strong dinosaur. It liked eating meat very much.

Tyrannosaurus rex

Triceratops

Tyrannosaurus rex wants to eat Triceratops!

**1** Which dinosaur had strong teeth?

Tyrannosaurus rex had strong teeth.

**2** Which dinosaur liked eating meat?

**3** Which dinosaur did Tyrannosaurus rex want to eat?

**12** **Look at the picture. Ask and answer questions with a friend.**

Little dinosaurs

Many dinosaurs were very small.

Velociraptor

Velociraptor was a small dinosaur. It liked eating meat, too.

14

**1** Was Velociraptor very big?

No, Velociraptor was very small.

**2** Did Velociraptor like meat?

**3** Did Velociraptor have claws?

**4** Was Velociraptor a beautiful animal?

## 13 Circle the correct picture.

**1** Which dinosaur's name begins with "Velo. . ."?

a

b

**2** Which dinosaur's name begins with "Tyranno. . ."?

a

b

**3** Who does not live on Earth now?

a

b

**4** Where can we see dinosaurs from the past?

a

b

**14** **Match the two parts of the phrase.**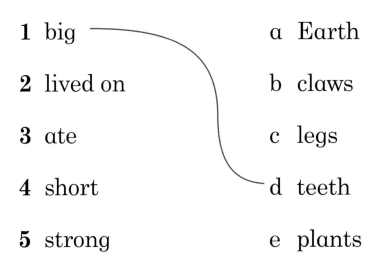

1 big             a Earth

2 lived on      b claws

3 ate            c legs

4 short        d teeth

5 strong      e plants

**15** **Look at the picture
and read the questions.
Write complete sentences.** 📖 ✏️

**1** When did dinosaurs live on Earth?

They lived on Earth in

the past.

**2** Are they on Earth now?

**3** Did they have teeth?

**16** **Look at the letters.**
**Write the words.**

1  d n s u s i o a r

Some children are frightened of

d i n o s a u r s .

2  w a l c s

Velociraptor had big, strong

T e e t h.

3  e l i v d

Dinosaurs L i v d e

in the past.

4  h E a r t

There are no dinosaurs

on E a r t h now.

**17** **Ask and answer the questions about dinosaurs with a friend.**

1

> Are you frightened of dinosaurs? Why? ~~I am~~ Why not?

> I am frightened of dinosaurs. They have got big teeth.

**2** What is your favorite dinosaur? Why?

**3** Do you like movies about dinosaurs?

**4** Do you like books about dinosaurs?

**5** Would you like to see dinosaurs from the past?

## 18 Do the crossword.

| | | | | | |
|---|---|---|---|---|---|
| ¹m | o | u | ²t | h | s |

³p

⁴s

## Across

**1** Dinosaurs put food in their . . .

**3** Some dinosaurs ate . . .

**4** Some dinosaurs liked fighting with their . . . claws.

## Down

**2** Some dinosaurs had strong . . . in their mouths

**3** Dinosaurs lived in the . . .

**19** **Circle the correct word.**

**1** Dinosaurs did not live

    **a** in zoos.        **b** on Earth.

**2** Dinosaurs were not

    **a** animals.        **b** birds.

**3** Dinosaurs had to find

    **a** food.        **b** towns.

**4** Some dinosaurs liked fighting

    **a** with cats.        **b** with their claws.

**5** Today, we can see dinosaurs

    **a** in zoos.        **b** from the past.

**20** **Read and write. Write *yes* or *no*.**

1  Triceratops liked
   eating meat.                      *yes* ~~~~

2  Tyrannosaurus rex was
   a small dinosaur.                 *no*

3  Velociraptor liked
   fighting.                         *yes*

4  Diplodocus had long legs.   *no*

5  Tyrannosaurus rex
   ate plants with its big,
   strong teeth.                     *no*

**21** **Complete the questions.**
**Write *Why*, *What*, or *When*.**

**1** _ What _ did Triceratops eat?

It ate plants.

**2** _ Why _ did dinosaurs fight for food?

Because they were hungry.

**3** _ Why _ did dinosaurs see on Earth?

They saw lots of big and small dinosaurs.

**4** _ why _ did dinosaurs live?

They lived in the past.

**5** _ Why _ did Tyrannosaurus rex have big, strong teeth?

Because he ate with them.

# Level 2

**The Gingerbread Man**

978-0-241-25442-4 ✓

**Sly Fox and Red Hen**

978-0-241-25443-1 ☒

**The Monster Next Door**

978-0-241-25444-8 →

**Wild Animals**

978-0-241-25445-5 ☒

**Little Red Riding Hood**

978-0-241-25446-2 ✓

**Dinosaurs**

978-0-241-25447-9 ✓

**Topsy and Tim The Big Race**

978-0-241-25448-6 ✓

**Goes to the Treehouse**

978-0-241-25449-3 ☒

**Sports Day**

978-0-241-26222-1 ✓

**Going on a Picnic**

978-0-241-26221-4 ☒

## Now you're ready for Level 3!

**Notes**
CEFR levels are based on guidelines set out in the Council of Europe's European Framework. Cambridge Young Learners English (YLE) Exams give a reliable indication of a child's progression in learning English.